HOW TO BE A DOG WALKER

A Pocket Guide

Jamie Shanks

CONTENTS

Title Page

Copyright

Introduction   1

Preparing To Start   3

Marketing Your Business   18

Being a Responsible Dog Walker   22

Advice on Building your Business   33

Things you'll need   39

Epilogue   47

First Aid for Dogs   54

treat recipe for dog walking   65

Dog Walking Contract   67

Pet and Owner's Info Sheet   71

Veterinary release form   73

Thank you for buying my book   75

Other Books By This Author   77

INTRODUCTION

May 10th, 2010

I sat on the train and watched the trees fly by as a jobless man. I had been unemployed for six months when I arrived at the job centre for the very last time. An hour later, and after sorting out some paperwork, I sat back on the train and watched the same scenery go by: the same trees, the same buildings, the same spring blue sky, yet my whole world had changed. I was now and suddenly a self-employed dog walker, and there was a future for me beckoning, good or bad.

With no clients, no car - just a bike - and no real idea what I was doing, I set out to walk one dog after another from 9 am - 5 pm. Lovely easy solo walks with the idea that I'd earn £50 if I could walk five dogs a day.

I built a website, made my logo, and marketed myself well. My website was ranking on Google, but I still had no clients.

But then, two weeks later, someone called to ask if I could walk their cocker spaniel named Jay - I was now a professional!

Jay (2011)

PREPARING TO START

Let's get down to business

The chances are high that you own a dog. In that case, you've no doubt been out walking at your go-to place and seen the local dog walkers arriving in their vans, taking their group out for a walk, and wished you could do the same. Spending time outdoors with dogs and getting paid for it seems almost too good to be true. Especially if you're not happy in your current job - I wonder if it's your job that made you buy this book?

Dog walkers are popping up everywhere, and all share the dream of finally earning a fair wage, in proper working conditions, and doing something they love. There's plenty of work out there, and you can be successful even with little to no funds to invest, but you must be 100% committed to make your new business work!

To make sure your business doesn't fail in the first few months, plan how you will pay your bills while you build a client base. If you have a partner or family that can support you, that's great. But if not, consider looking for evening and weekend work to bring in extra income while leaving the daytime available for dog walking. An evening job like a takeaway driver is ideal.

The first thing you should do is research your local dog walkers. So get on Google and Facebook and find all your local dog walkers in your area. Find out what their prices are like and what services they offer.

Areas vary slightly, so London prices are different from the rest of the UK, and even one town can have different prices from the town next to it. Find the average price the locals are charging and set that price as yours. For example, walking a dog for an hour where I live is around £10-£12 with discounts for secondary dogs from the same home.

There are two types of dog walks - group and solo. Most people are happy to get their dog walked in a group, so they get to socialise and play. You can charge more money for a solo walk, but you get paid way more money walking six dogs in a group than one dog on its own. A couple of group walks a day can be enough for a dog walker to make a living. Some do just that - it makes for an ideal job for those who have kids and want to work during school hours.

So what is the main reason someone hires a dog walker? Answer: They're usually at work. I didn't know this when I started, and I just hoped someone would pay me to walk their dog. I didn't even consider the motivation of those that hire a dog walker. Who wants to give their money away, after all? Dog walking for most dog owners is enjoyable. So for most clients, it's a necessity, as in there's no one else at home to do it. And because the most common need for a dog walker is that the owner is at work, nearly everyone wants their dog walked in the middle of the working day. Not 9 am just after they've left home and not 5 pm when they're on their way back. So the lunchtime period is peak working hours for a dog walker. You may only manage two walks at that time (an early lunch walk and a late lunch walk. Eg. 11 am & 1 pm). You will earn most of your money for the day during lunch, so you can't do solo walks or offer any other service during this time – that time is for group walks only.

I'm not saying you shouldn't do solo walks. You may get asked to do walks by people like the elderly and the disabled who don't mind what time their dogs get walked during the day; as long as they get walked - you can fit them around your schedule. But solo walks tend to be done more by those just starting with time on their hands, while the established dog walkers tend to stick to group walks only. For example, I walk three group walks a day, and then I'm done.

You'll be surprised how much time it takes to pick up and drop off dogs. Taking three groups of dogs out for a 1-hour walk takes me around 6 hours – half my working day is collecting or dropping dogs off – in a small area. Dog walkers are always racing against the clock, so working in a small area is always advisable.

Potiphar and Chilli getting picked up for a walk

Decide what services to offer

The most popular services are doggy daycare, dog boarding, and cat visits outside of dog walking. Doggy daycare is taking off nowadays. Dogs come to stay with you for the day (or half-day) while their owners are at work, with usually the option of a pick-up and drop-off service available. I don't offer daycare, but it's a significant rival/addition to dog walking and growing by the day. You can charge quite a bit more for daycare, but someone will have to be at home to look after the pups if you are out dog walking. Some dog walkers offer this service, and some folks provide daycare exclusively. There are dedicated premises for larger daycare centres that also hire staff.

When looking for a dog walker, clients will sometimes look for those that can board their dogs, too – this is quite important to some, but it's not a deal-breaker. People like to go on holiday or the odd weekend away, so having a dog walker that can look after their dog is a big bonus, plus boarding pays well (£20-£30+ per night, per dog). In the summer months and school holidays, a dog walker's wage can almost double with the addition of the boarders, but it can be hard work. Expect to wake up to 'accidents'. Several dogs living with you can bring a lot of dirt and fur into the house and along the walls - your once beautiful lawn is now scorched with urine.

Skye on her first puppy walk (2011)

Apart from group dog walking, dog boarding, and

doggy daycare, all other services are just pocket money. If you don't fancy them, it's OK to forget about them, including pet sitting cats and other furries. But what is Pet Sitting? Do you know? I've been doing this for 12 years, and I sometimes wonder. Is it cat visits? Is it dog sitting in the owner's home or dog boarding in yours? Is it something to do with caged pets? Well, it's all those things actually and more. Technically, Pet Sitting is an umbrella term. Any pet that is cared for in either their own home or your home is Pet Sitting. It's a vague term, and I wouldn't say I like it, as it can mean anything to anyone. So if you do promote Pet Sitting as a service, then describe what it is you're offering to potential clients. Think about how your potential clients will feel if you list it as a service alongside cat visits and dog sitting, as I often see. I prefer only to list actual pet sitting services I offer, e.g., cat visits and dog boarding. But whatever services you offer, describe clearly what each service is in layman's terms, and don't just assume clients will know. Most are hoping you will explain what you do, how you do it, and what it will cost them.

Quote: "You've got your hands full!" and "You must be fit!" are the two most common phrases you'll hear from the public, day after day.

Elsa and Jack are boarding at my house

Learn basic canine first aid

Caring for someone's cherished pet is an enormous responsibility. Walking a single dog on a lead is usually a carefree walk, but walking six dogs off lead in a public place with distractions is another matter. Therefore, we must remain 100% focused and on the lookout for problems and potential problems.

You will learn that you have to see problems before they arise, and for most, this will come naturally and with experience. For example, if one of your dogs is prone to running over to greet other people's dogs, it's up to you to see that dog before your dog does and respond accordingly. Likewise, if you have a male who doesn't like other males or likes to hump other males, you have to see that other male first and move away, put your dog on a lead, or distract him.

When approaching other people and their dogs, I always look for the owner's body language first. Do they look nervous seeing me and the dogs approach? Are they relaxed and happy? Is their dog on lead or off? Being alert and seeing problems before they arise is the first rule of canine first aid – preventing injury.

I've been lucky that no dog I walk has ever suffered from severe injury – sure, I've seen the odd cut pad, broken toenail, but I haven't had to deal with much! But I'm always cautious as something can happen in a split second that results in injury, resulting in substantial vet bills.

A first aid course will teach you how to treat injured dogs in an emergency. From bleeding to choking, dealing with broken bones, and even CPR and heart massage – this will give you peace of mind and a good selling point to clients.

With experience, I've learned that it's usually the same dogs that will injure themselves repeatedly rather than random members of the group. It's always those same dogs that run the most that get the sprains, cut pads, or worse – hypoglycemia! I explained this to the editor of Country Walking magazine in 2016 when I helped him write an article about hiking with your dog.

Hypoglycaemia is when the dog's sugar levels drop after they push themselves too hard – I've seen it happen within 30 minutes of a walk. If a dog is not used to much activity, it's more common than a regularly exercised dog. They become lethargic and dizzy, it can be pretty dangerous, so I always have some honey in my first aid kit just in case, but it's scarce. It's happened to me twice, and it's always those same dogs that want to run after every ball, chase after everything, and do it all as fast as possible. You have to be their brakes because they won't stop, and usually, the working breeds are guilty of this.

An excellent simple precaution is not to push the dog harder than it gets at home. Sure, let the dogs play, have fun, and tire themselves out, but in moderation. Clients' dogs may only get one long walk a day or long walks only on weekends, so I give them timeouts throughout the walk if it's a highly charged one. The last dog that went hypo on a walk did so, trying to keep up with my super fit Springer Spaniel, but I carried a 30-kilo dog back to the van. But like I said, it's infrequent, and you will probably never experience it.

Dog walking isn't all the 'Sunshine and rainbows' that some think it is and, at times, can be pretty stressful. But learning some basic first aid will make your life a lot easier and take a lot of the anxiety away. It could be the difference between life and death for the pet in your care! Get to know a dog behaviourist! They can be pretty easy to find on Google in your local area. Learning and understanding some dog behaviour basics is beneficial for a dog walker. Even if you are an experienced dog owner, it will make a big difference. It's pretty easy to reinforce lousy behaviour; simply giving the behaviour attention can be enough to make it worse! Understanding why a dog is doing what it does can be essential and help you learn about the dog you are walking. How would you deal with it if a new dog joined the group, but one of the other dogs didn't like it, or there were group issues?

Tip: In an emergency, you can take the dog to any vet (meaning the closest at hand), not just their registered vet. All that vet needs to know is what clinic the dog's registered with so they can get their info. Vets will also treat injured wild animals should you come across any.

Get Insurance and sort out the paperwork

You'll need to get pet business insurance to protect yourself from any liabilities. There are quite a few around and easy to find online. Two big companies are 'Pet Businesses Insurance' and 'Cliverton' with many others online. It should cost about £15-£20 a month. Insurance covers replacing locks of clients' homes should their keys be lost or stolen. And covers vet bills should the animal you are looking after come to harm through your negligence. Also, insurance will generally (or optionally) cover other pet services like dog boarding, daycare, pet taxi, etc. When taking on new clients, dog walkers need three primary forms: A 'Dog Walking Contract,' A 'Pet and Owner's Info Sheet,' and a 'Vet Release Form.' The

Dog Walking Contract is the agreement between the dog walker and the client. The Pet and Owner's Info Sheet contains owner contact details and pet info. Finally, the Vet Release Form may be the most important as it gives you the power to take the dog to the vet and agree to their treatment. A vet can't do much for an injured dog without consent. They are liable should something happen without it, so they can only offer the most basic treatment.

Tip: I've often had emails from dog walkers unable to get their vehicles insured for dog walking. Not many insurance companies want to take us on. So if you are having trouble, try Hastings.

You have to register your dog walking business with HMRC to pay taxes on your income. You can earn around £10,000 a year before starting paying tax. By law, you have to keep your financial records up to date, so everything that's coming in and going out. Hence, an accountant is worthwhile and relatively cheap. But it's pretty easy to do yourself. Taxes are done online every January on the HMRC website, and you are paying tax for the previous year.

Using either spreadsheet software or a notepad, write down every time a client pays you, whether daily, weekly, or monthly, for each month – this is your incomings. For outgoings, you are looking at fuel bills, van insurance, dog walking insurance, dog leads, cages, and treats. So it's not complicated.

Online, HRMC will only ask you for your incoming and outgoing total for the year and then work out what you owe in tax.

Some people will be entitled to working tax credits to help top up their earnings (I was) so check into that as the income can help when you start.

You might want to get a business bank account too. They are similar to your personal bank account but used just for business. It makes it easier to keep track of your incomings and outgoings and doesn't cost anything.

Since you will generally get a key to the owner's home while they're out, it's best to have a certificate showing you have been Police checked (DRB/CRB check).

Letting strangers in their homes alone is a big deal for most people. That is why dog walkers rely so heavily on recommendations. If their friend or someone they know trusts you, they are far more likely to choose you than someone unknown. Disclosure Scotland is a government-run organisation and can offer disclosure certificates to anyone in the UK. But you can Google to find others that provide the same service.

Choosing a business name

There's more to think about in a business name than you might think. If you plan to work alone, then a more personal business name may suit you better as pet care is a very personal service. I'm known locally as Jamie, the dog walker, and people recommend using that term, so if I needed to start all over again, that could be a suitable business name.

There has also been quite a benefit of using your location in your business name. It made it much easier to rank in Google search. Around 2011-2012 if you Googled for a dog walker using my location, my website, and all the directories it listed on took up the whole first page. But now, I only appear once, like most others do, with maybe my Facebook page listing. Google has changed a lot since those days. Google keeps tweaking its algorithms to improve user experience, so there is a chance that adding your location to your business name may become redundant.

If I planned to start a pet business and hire helpers as it grew, calling my business "Jamie's dog walking" doesn't make much sense. Nor does it o offer other pet services, like cat visits and small animal boarding. So for those with ambitions and plans of hiring staff, a less personal, more inclusive name is better. For example, if I started again and wanted a team and offered a spectrum of pet services, a business name like "Bishopton Pet Nannies" would make more sense. It includes the location and the term "pet" rather than just "dog" but also has the plural "Nannies," letting people know there is more than just me working there.

Since pet care can be so personal, some people won't use businesses that hire staff. They want to choose their pet person and have them walk their dog or care for their pet. Also, those who hire staff can struggle to keep them for long. It pays poorly, hours are low, and it isn't as fun as it sounds. Yet, because of the appeal of working with pets, businesses never have trouble getting new staff. Still, their clients have to get used to a new dog walker becoming common every so often.

After four years, I hired someone as I found myself overbooked and told some clients their dogs would get walked by my new helper, and most were ok. But some didn't like the idea of someone they didn't know or trust walking their dog or coming into their home. So what I learned is that if you hire help and then pass some clients onto your team, it can make some clients feel disgruntled: the agreement of terms has now changed.

So my advice is, if you get a helper, then give them the new dogs to walk, not current dogs. New clients will be happy to have your helper walk their dog from the start.

Monday's early lunch gang visit the beach

Get a logo

A logo can help build your business identity. There are a few ways to get one:

- Pay a graphic artist to make you one – expensive
- Create one yourself
- Steal one from the internet
- Buy a premade logo from a stock website
- Visit Fiverr.com - cheaper

MARKETING YOUR BUSINESS

Getting noticed online

If you want an online presence, a Facebook business page may be all you need. But a website can also help. Those who don't know of any dog walkers will likely Google for one and find local businesses (and their websites) listed. Register on 'Google Business.' Doing this will list your business (and website) on local search results and Google maps – a must-do action, and it's free! But remember, it's not about being number one on Google; it's about building an effective website that turns visitors into clients - this is marketing.

Half of my work comes from Facebook and the other half from my website, and primarily at the beginning, when I had no word of mouth, all of it came from my website. But 2010 was a different time with no Facebook.

There are loads of dog walking websites that rank high on Google, but their sites are hopeless. They will never convert visitors to clients, so make sure that you give the visitor what they want straight away if you have a website. Too many sites focus on talking about themselves when they should be letting visitors know what they can do for them - all people care about is what you can do for them!

On the website, state clearly what services you offer, what areas you work in, your prices, and how to contact you. Lay down the simple facts, and explain how it all works. People are lazy online; bullet points make for easy reading. It's not about you. It's about what you can do for the client!

I advertise my dog walking services in Erskine and Bishopton, and I state that on the first line of my website – that tells visitors what I do and where. I then list how it works in bullet points, and underneath that, I have a 'call to action' (CTA). A CTA is a directive used in marketing campaigns. It tells the visitor what we want them to do next. People expect to be led by the hand online.

Some CTA examples:

- Sign up to start your free trial.
- Buy one pizza, get one free! Order now!
- Get your dog walked! Call Today!

Since we want them to contact us, we'll add our CTA telling them to do so on every website page.

Tip: When you walk a new dog for the first time, it's important to post photos to Facebook that same day (if possible). You can bet your bottom dollar that your new client will be visiting your Facebook page aplenty that first day because the new client wants reassurance. Most are anxious when a stranger takes their dog out for the first time. Photos let clients see for themselves that all is good. Posting photos to Facebook is ideal for reassuring and giving an excellent impression to new clients. Not to do so is to keep your client's insecurities lingering – this can cause resentment and potentially for the client to find another, more reassuring dog walker.

My van with logo

Advertise your business on your vehicle

An excellent advertising method is to get stickers on your vehicle if you have one. Then, hundreds of people will see you every day, and it doesn't cost much. Anywhere you park, outside your house, outside a client's home, or in the supermarket is advertising for your business.

BEING A RESPONSIBLE DOG WALKER

Always be in control

Control is what dog walking is all about and the most important thing to remember. Being in control is the number one rule. It's more important than giving the dogs a good run and play. More important than letting them pee and poo. If you're in control, dogs are safe. If you're not, then they're not.

You have to be able to control the dogs you walk and what that means is that dogs off the lead should stay close to you, come when called, and be focused on you. The easiest way to control dogs is to be the centre of attention and even give the dogs a job to do. That might mean using a ball to keep the focus for some, retrieving things from the water for others or just having playmates. However you do it, the dog must know that being with you is better than being away from you. Else they are likely to entertain themselves. What's happening over there may look a lot more fun. That means they are running away to greet other dogs, that means they are following a scent they've found, that means you are not in control.

Being the centre of attention is the number one mega secret of being a good dog walker. Unfortunately, not many dog walkers understand this, so I'll repeat it, **you are the centre of attention**. It's more fun for dogs to be with you than away from you – play with them – entertain them – talk to them, don't ignore them - give them a job to do – remember that, and you will be doing well!

If all else fails, they go on the lead. As I said, I've said this to many dog walkers who can't stop their dogs from running off. Still, they don't seem to get it for some reason, and eventually, most of their dogs end up permanently on lead.

Out on a walk and I have their full attention!

Introducing new dogs to the group

Try to know as much about the new dog before you walk it. Are they dog-friendly? If not neutered, does it get on well with other males? If it's a female, is it spayed? Are there any breeds they don't like or anything you need to be made aware of? If you want, you can organise for the owner and dog to join you for a walk with your group so they can meet first.

Sometimes owners won't tell you what you really should know because they count on you to walk their dog, but there can be signs that can give you insight if you look closely. For example, if they have a bungee lead, they might not be goon on lead. This can also be true if they use a harness or head collar. If they have an extendable lead, the dog probably doesn't get off lead much, find out why.

Outside where dogs can run free and have plenty

of room, they can ignore the other dogs if they're not happy in their company. But in the vehicle, dogs won't ignore each other. So any problems will surface in the vehicle. New dogs always need to be placed in a separate area from the rest – this is why you need a minimum of two spaces in your vehicle.

Usually, dogs are fine, young puppies are always good, but the most likely scenario you'll find is from the males and non socialised dogs. Unneutered males don't always like other males, especially complete males, but this isn't always the case. Some males do need neutering but haven't been, and they can cause problems with other males, harass and get too personal towards the girls and cause trouble. Some dog walkers (not many) only walk female dogs because of this.

If you have a complete female, you'll have to let the owner know that you can't take them on group walks when they are in season. However, you might be able to offer a solo walk which would have to be on the lead.

Suppose a dog hasn't been socialised enough at a young age. It really might not like being in proximity to other dogs in the vehicle, but a separate area can remedy that.

Your dogs must be dog and people friendly! Most dog owners will tell you their dog is friendly. Whether they are or not is another matter. If their dog doesn't want anything to do with other dogs but doesn't go for them, you may expect to hear that it's friendly! Dog walking can be pretty funny that way, and some owners are, let's say, very loyal towards their dogs. So unless it's a puppy, you will have to find out what the dog is like.

You could have a fantastic team filled with lovely sociable dogs having a great time together, all under your control. Then you bring in a new dog that profoundly changes the dynamic of that walk for the worse. For me, dogs that cause problems in the group are the worst part of dog walking. Suppose I come across a dog that doesn't fit in enough because it's too hard to control or not friendly. I will let the owner know that its' not working out and end that dog's time with us - for the good of the group walk.

Regarding new dogs, it should only take a couple of walks for you to get a good idea of how that dog is and how it gets on with the pack. Even after one walk, you should have a reasonable idea.

The pack on a beach walk

Don't let dogs off lead until you are ready

You learn when you can let a dog off the lead with experience, but I can offer some great tips and advice on when to let the dog off the lead for the first time.

Some dogs will happily walk with you off the lead on their first walk and come to you when you call them but not all! Puppies are generally the easiest. Second to pups are the dogs familiar with getting walked by different people or have had a dog walker in the past. But the older the dog gets, the more time it can take to adjust to new things. So older dogs that have never had a dog walker usually need the most time – but that is not always the case.

You might be on a group walk with the new dog on the lead, and it shows signs of wanting to play with the group – this is a good sign but not enough. They might be keen on their pack mates, but they must also be keen on you. If they're not, they won't come back to you, respond well to your commands, or let you come close enough to them to put them back on the lead.

So you are looking for signs that they are comfortable with the other dogs and, more importantly, happy with you. Warnings that tell you they must stay on lead are:

- They are not pleased to see you when you arrive
- They are not happy with you in their home
- They won't take a treat from you (at home or on

a walk)
- Or they do take a treat but spit it back out.
- They respond poorly to your commands/ignore you
- They are nervous around their new group mates
- They are not keen on you touching them while they are on lead

The last sign is vital. If dogs don't like you touching them while on a lead, you will not get anywhere near them if you let them off, so you must keep them on. Thankfully trust builds quickly, and dogs learn that it's a walk, and they get to go back home afterwards, so it might be scary at first, but they soon get used to it. If they have a good time, it can take just a couple of walks, but if you're unsure, keep them on the lead until they get to know you better. Again, the older dogs are more prone to this than the younger ones (not always, though).

If you get a nervous dog, it generally just takes a few walks with the same pack for them to relax soon. However, if you have an unsure dog, it's crucial that you become Mr/Miss Chilled. No drama, loud voices, nothing that makes them think being walked by you or being in the group is wrong – make it a great thing!

Tip: When out and about and meeting people walking their dogs, chat with them as human and not as a potential client. Don't try to be a salesperson trying to get work, forcing your business cards down their throat. By just being friendly and chatty and without any agenda you build trust amongst people and should they need a dog walker they will choose you. Why? Cause you are someone they've gotten to know, a nice person to chat too and someone they trust.

Don't let the dogs be a nuisance

When walking dogs in public while they are off the lead, dogs need to behave in a particular manner and not bother or upset other people and their dogs. You can get a bad reputation that can spread quickly on social media.

With social media, we get something called 'call-out' culture. An opportunity for someone to gain prestige and status by shaming others publicly. If you're a regular on Facebook or Twitter, you'll see it now and again. Since you can get prestige from a 'call-out', there is much motivation from certain types to do this if given a chance.

A good few years back, I was 'called out' when a stranger decided to kick a full-size football into the river for one of my dogs. Since the football was too big to get into the dog's mouth, the dog just pushed it further and further into the river, ignoring my commands to return and soon was far out. It was a terrifying experience, but she returned, oblivious to the drama. After that, all was fine until I saw later that a witness decided to post about it on the local community group on Facebook.

A close call was when I was walking with a client,

and her dog suddenly lunged at a passerby's dog. Outraged, the owner demanded to know if this was a dog from my pack. I replied, "No," and backed off. When the owner realised it was just a person out walking their dog rather than a pro dog walker, she quickly calmed down, and they were both chatting and laughing moments later. She changed that quick.

The response would have been very different if that dog was under my control. Maybe a bad review, perhaps a Facebook rant, but whatever the reaction would have been, it would not be nearly as forgiving since I'm a professional. Since we get paid, are professionals, own a business, offer a service, people have the right to complain. They are entitled to shame us, wag their finger at us, and even shout. This is why so many dog walkers look for quiet areas to walk the dogs away from the public.

Ok, so here are some rules for how dogs should behave in public:

• Dogs need to stay close to you, not running about all over the place. They can run after a ball as long as they come straight back. If your dogs are all close, this is reassuring to people that they are under control, which puts their minds at rest. As soon as any dog wanders, I call it back, it's second nature for me, and now my dogs stick to me like glue unless I throw a ball for them. But if I'm on a path and a bike comes, I can walk off the path taking all the dogs with me to let the cyclist pass.

• Don't let dogs run as a group toward other people's dogs. Very intimidating.
• Don't let your males hump or try to dominate other people's dogs.
• Don't let your dogs surround another dog that you pass.
• Don't let your dogs steal other dogs' toys or chase after them.
• Dogs should be seen and not heard. Some dogs are very loud, particularly when excited. Not acceptable for a public place if it's continuous. I've let dogs go because of how loud they were.
• Dogs should focus on you, reassuring the public that they are under control.

Pack Culture

Packs have their own culture, every walk may have a slightly different culture from the next, but the gap is more prominent between dog walkers. For example, it might mean throwing one ball for all six dogs on one walk, one ball for each dog on another, or letting them all play amongst themselves or it could be lead walks for all the dogs. By culture, I mean the learned group social behaviour of dogs on that particular walk.

So my packs are inward-facing, which means they focus on me and their fellow packmates, which is what I want. When new dogs join the group, they adopt this culture, and it's easier for them to do this when they are young. So the pack is like a bubble, and what is happening outside of the bubble is irrelevant and ignored.

Some other dog walkers have outward-facing packs. That means what is happening over there is a lot more interesting. So when new dogs join that group, they adopt that culture and become focused on what's happening outside the pack.

I've seen this before years ago with another dog walker whose own dog felt threatened by other people and always ran over to other people's dogs. It was always on the lookout for something. What was that noise? Who's that in the distance? What's that smell? Is this a threat? The whole pack soon adopted that behaviour.

I ended up with some of their dogs, and it took weeks of work to bring them back into 'the bubble' and lose focus on what was happening over there.

ADVICE ON BUILDING YOUR BUSINESS

Offer puppy services to bring in new clients

It will take time for your businesses to pick up, but it will. Don't mistake thinking that you'll get an instant response once you set up your Facebook page or make a website. Everyone who needs a dog walker already has one they trust, and they aren't going to chuck them because some Joe claims that they'll do it a £1 less! It's the people that will need a dog walker in the future that will be your clients.

When you advertise, the people interested most likely don't need you right now. They might need you in a few weeks when they get that new puppy or in a month when they go back to work. So you have to see it as an investment when it comes to advertising – you advertise now, but the results come later. So be patient, and don't go expecting instant results the same day you advertise.

And on that note, why not offer puppy services such as puppy visits? Two visits a day (outside of the lunchtime walks, say 10 am and 2 pm) for a tenner (or a twenty) and soon that pup will be a dog and on your walks with the rest. Unfortunately, established dog walkers tend to be too busy to afford the time to give to puppies. However, new businesses do have the time, so I recommend promoting your puppy services and posting lots of gorgeous puppy pics on Facebook.

Why not even offer to take the puppy on your group walks to get them socialised? That's what I did, partly because I didn't have the time for puppy visits once I became established. But I know what you're thinking. Pups are too young for group walks, you say! Bones are still growing! Then get a puppy carrier and carry the puppy on the walk! I did that first with my pup, then with clients' puppies, and it works great. They will become socialised and find confidence in their new world while they are at that very impressionable age – even when carried. I was taught this trick by my behaviourist and recommend it.

But for all new dog walking startups out there, I expect to see your puppy services heavily promoted on a Facebook page.

Elsa getting a pup visit in 2013

Don't take on too many part-time dogs

Most of your income will come from dog walking (boarding and daycare) (even though cat visits will bring in some pocket money). So your most valuable dogs are going to be the 'full-time' dogs you walk Monday – Friday, with 'shift' dogs making up the rest of your dog walking clients.

Shift dogs are the dogs you only get a few days a week, depending on the work shift patterns of clients. Those days will be either the same days week in, week out or different each week, and some weeks they won't need you. The problem with those dogs is that you will get close to being fully booked on some days or even overbooked. And on other days, you will only have your full-time dogs leaving you half empty! The problem with shift dogs is that you're limited to the possibility of being full rather than being full. So I'd be wary of taking on too many.

Tip: When approaching a person walking with their dog, look at the body language of the dog owner to find out if that dog is friendly or not. If the owner is relaxed, chances are the dog is friendly, but if they react to you and the pack, act accordingly and avoid any issues.

Elsa and Brodie play

Be honest

Don't ever lie to clients. We all make mistakes, and we have to accept that. You forget to walk a dog or get the days mixed up. It happens. But whatever happens, clients cant judge too harshly on your mistakes and are more likely to judge you on how you respond. So whatever happens, be honest and don't ever try to cover things up. You may lose a client, but this usually depends on how long you've had the dog.

Trust is like a points system. You start at zero with a new client and earn points overtime for being reliable and trustworthy. You score more points from the client knowing the dog is bonding with you and the client knowing their dog is having a good time, e.g. Facebook photos, a pleasant reaction from the dog when you arrive.

You will lose points if you forget a walk. Therefore long-established dogs are the safest and have the most points. New dogs have the least, so losing points early on could mean losing that client. You have to put it down to experience and carry on if it happens. It doesn't happen much, but if you do forget to walk a dog, it's usually because you were to walk a dog on a day or time it's not usually walked on. It hurts, you worry your good reputation will take a beating, but it won't, and your business will be fine.

So never lie. You will not see your business go down the pan by forgetting to walk a dog – we all make mistakes, and people understand that. But lying about it is another matter. If you lie to cover it up and get caught out, the damage could be way worse. Dog walking is about trust. Making a mistake doesn't mean you're not trustworthy but lying about it does.

Also, to be blunt and honest with you, what people think, what the public thinks and what ex-clients think doesn't matter compared to what your current clients think. The public could not like you, but as long as your clients think you're amazing, that's the most important thing. They pay you, and their money pays your bills, no one else's.

Tip: For new dogs, it's important to post photos to Facebook that same day (if possible). You can be sure your new client will be visiting your Facebook page aplenty that first day because they want reassurance. Most are anxious when a stranger takes their dog out for the first time. Posting photos on Facebook is an ideal way to reassure new clients. Not doing so can cause resentment and potentially the client hiring someone else.

THINGS YOU'LL NEED

Be properly equipped to walk dogs

You'll need a few things when out dog walking. At least six dog leads, all the same type and length. You don't want to use the client's leads as they vary in size, from chain leads to extendable leads to super short leads. This makes trying to walk them all on the lead very hard. Imagine having six dogs on the lead with four on short leads and two on leads just long enough that they can still play – they will weave in and out, left to right, and soon you'll have a tangled mess! If you plan to do group walks off-lead like me, you still need to have dogs on a lead at the start when taking them out of the vehicle and at the end when taking them back.

Avoid clip leads. If they get dirty, the clip jams, and you can't open it. Chain leads will rust. Now I use only rope leads as they are very quick to put on a dog, plus when they get filthy, you just put them in the washing machine. I'd never use a clip lead now.

If you buy rope leads (slip leads), then get the chunky type (10mm-12mm in thickness). The slim type can cut into your hands if the dog is a puller and brutal on winter days when your hands are cold. 'Figure of 8' dog leads are great if you are worried about a group of dogs pulling you off your feet as they prevent the dogs from pulling and can be used as standard slip leads. Still, I don't recommend rope leads for pups or those that pull too hard.

You are responsible only for the dogs you walk. Still, you might find your wee group attracts other dogs to come over, and they may or may not be friendly. Hence, a rope lead means you can whip it over any dogs that may be troublesome, even if that dog doesn't have a collar and be in control of that dog before anything happens.

Poo bags are essential – you don't want a £60 fine for not picking it up or a tarnished reputation. Instead, you can buy baby nappy(diaper) bags as they cost a fraction of the price of poo bags. On hot days you might need to take water with you.

And let's not forget how essential treats are. Treats are great for teaching dogs to come when you call them. Also, it's a good habit to give them a treat when you pick them up, so they quickly see your arrival as a good thing. Treats make things a lot easier, and I can't think of a better treat for dogs than dried liver (recipe at the end of the book). Every dog I've ever walked would walk on hot coals for a liver tit-bit. Forget buying treats; they are expensive, and you'll go through several packs a week.

You should be able to let most dogs off the lead, so you might want to take a tennis ball and a ball launcher - Chuckit makes the best and will last a long time. Now that I walk dogs in groups, I find that some dogs like to play with other dogs, but some will always want just to play ball.

Suppose the dog comes across animal poo like fox or deer or a dead animal, then there's a good chance they will roll in it. It's pretty disgusting, and the smell is just awful. Dogs love rolling in poo and always find a way of getting dirty, but you can't take them home like that, so if you are walking at places where there is no river or lake to clean them in, you need some way to clean them up. A pump-action porta shower is perfect and requires no electricity, and you can clean them up and then dry them in the van or back home.

And if you want to save yourself much time, then a doggy bathrobe is very handy, wrap it over a wet dog, and it will help dry them while you're driving them home. I bought some for clients and have a few myself.

You're going to end up with many keys to clients' homes. I've got about 30 keys in my possession, maybe more. It's easy to lose keys, so keep them all together. I use a large screw gate carabiner, and it resembles something a prison warden would keep. All the keys are safe in one place. I've only ever lost a key once, and it was a key that I yet hadn't added to my carabiner. They are small and easy to lose.

I used to put dog name tags on all my keys, and if you can keep the keys safe, it helps remind you whose key is whose. Now I don't use tags and remember from memory.

I use a large screw gate carabiner to keep all the keys safe

Preparing your vehicle for dogs

You can use a car or a van. Some even use a hatchback with the back seats down. Estates are reasonably common, and many will start with a car but then upgrade to a van later. Of course, a van is better but costs more to buy and kit out.

The first thing I did with previous cars was to get stickers put on them, tint the windows, and create two separate areas for the dogs. If you have a car, tinting the windows is a good idea as it hides the dogs.

I now use two large 42-inch cages in my Berlingo (other dog walkers may have smaller cages and more of them). But in past cars, I split the dogs between the back seats and the boot. If using a car, keep the dogs in the back seats safe by avoiding them getting into the front as you drive. To do that, place a 'front seat dog guard' to block the gap between the front seats and then place a dog guard behind the front headrests, and the front is now secure. Next, put another dog guard behind the rear headrests, and you now have two separate and protected areas for the dogs. Of course, you need at least two places in your vehicle if you get one dog that needs its own space, which you will!

Next, I'd add some front seat covers and a dog hammock on the back seats to stop the back seats from getting wrecked.

Finally, I'd fit wind deflectors for the front side windows. It can be a struggle to dry the inside of the vehicle entirely, and in winter, it never really dries out. Wind deflectors allow me always to keep the windows open just a little. They are open 24 hours a day, even if it's pouring outside, and no one can see that gap as the deflectors hide it, rain can't get in, and the airflow allows the car to dry overnight. Without them, the interior smells like an old laundry basket by the next day, and things inside begin to corrode

My old Chevrolet estate was always damp inside, and while on a walk, the headlights came on by themselves. Then after starting the car and taking the key out, the car kept on running, and then it began to smoke from the electrics. I had to disconnect the battery to get the car to stop.

If you have a van, installing cages is easy, but a custom-made cage setup is a way if you have the money and want the best.

Keep the inside reasonably clean and sanitised. Suppose you have a dozen or more dogs in your vehicle a day. It just takes one dog with kennel cough to cause an outbreak.

Wear suitable clothing

You'll need the right clothes, waterproofs, woolly hats, gloves and general outdoor gear. For me, clothing is all about three things. Apart from my car and my camera I have spent more money on these three things than anything else: Jackets, bags and wellies for the wet. Get them right and prepared. Get them wrong, and you can spend hundreds trying to find the right gear. The rest of your clothing isn't a big deal. It's all about usability, durability and weight.

Winnie and Dior in the woods

After 3-4 hours of walking, your back aches, your

bag is digging into your neck, everything you are wearing is heavy, and when you get home, you want to throw all that weight off and relax. So you want things that work, durable but as light as possible.

You'll need a good bag with different departments to keep dirty, wet, slobbery tennis balls in one area. The dog leads in another, and maybe a drink. I prefer hunting/game bags. You can keep tennis balls and anything else that's wet and dirty in the mesh front and away from the leads and anything else you want to stay dry.

Regarding a jacket, the best ones are long in length with hoods – like the parka. They will keep you clean from jumping dogs, warm you, and have plenty of big pockets. Whatever you choose, I recommend length to your jacket to protect you from jumping dogs, lots of dirt, cold winds and rain. But in heavy rain, you'll find that most, if not all jackets are only water-resistant for a time and not waterproof. It doesn't matter if they are Goretex or waxed. If you are out for hours, then water will find a way in, plus walking dogs quickly ruin your clothes, so there is no point spending a fortune if you can get it right for less.

In all-day rain, staying dry makes life a lot more comfortable, and the only genuine jackets that are waterproof are jackets made from PVC. Dog walking isn't very fashionable, but you'll soon learn that you don't care if what you use works.

Last is the dog walker's best friend: a good pair of wellies. I always wear wellies when it's wet and have worn dozens of different brands. Wellies are a big deal to dog walkers, and many go through many pairs trying to find a pair that lasts. They are better than hiking boots because dog walking is much dirtier and wetter than hiking. Wellies are better at keeping you cleaner and drier around dogs, especially on muddy walks.

There are many rubbish pairs out there, many fancy brands that won't last, and I've bought them all. Poorly made wellies will only last a couple of weeks, good ones can last a year, and that's a good life for a dog walker's wellies. The company that makes the best and longest-lasting wellies are Dunlop – not the most fashionable brand, but they are genuine working wellies.

Tip: All day exposure to the elements, dry the skin and lips. I use a shea butter-based moisturiser and lip balm every morning to prevent the skin from weathering. Shea butter is weather-resistant, so it helps preserve our youthful looks.

EPILOGUE

Dealing with Kennel Cough outbreaks

Kennel cough is an 'umbrella term' or 'catch-all' term for any contagious canine respiratory disease. It's the canine equivalent of flu in humans and is usually very contagious. Dogs will be contagious before symptoms show and thus spread it to other dogs before any dog has shown any signs. Dogs can also contract it by being in close contact with where another contagious dog has been, e.g. sniffing the same post and playing with the same ball.

A dog that gets it could have contracted it a week before. It is challenging to stop it from entering the pack. All you can do and are responsible for is how you react to it. Now it's usually very mild, and if it breaks out in your pack, it will result most likely in this scenario:

- Most dogs won't get it.
- A substantial amount will have a mild cough and recover in a few days.
- One or two may need to see a vet for antibiotics.

Like humans, winter is respiratory disease season for dogs. Thankfully it's not that common. It shouldn't be an annual occurrence. In twelve years, I've encountered kennel cough only a few times. The first time it spread, the sick dogs stayed at home, and I walked the healthy dogs. But it made its way through the pack and lasted a good few weeks till it was gone. Two dogs needed to see a vet for antibiotics and recovered well. The rest recovered in just a few days, and more than half never got it or were asymptomatic.

The second time I went to pick up a dog, I noticed it had a cough and told the owner it couldn't come on the walk with the other dogs, that's all it took to stop it, and it never spread. Kennel cough would have been incubating in that dog for days, so a lucky escape.

Owners are scared of the term 'kennel cough', and one reason is that sick dogs and vet bills go together. You can't stop it from entering the pack. You can only take responsibility for how you respond to it. The worst response is to ignore it and let it spread. If you collect a dog with a cough, contact the owner and leave it at home or walk it alone. Maybe that is all it will take to stop any spread. If not, cancel all walks immediately for at least one week and ensure all have recovered and none show any signs before returning. Spray the van with disinfectant, wash all leads, and wash jackets. When you return to work, all should be fine.

Feeding a dog a diet to boost its immune system is recommended over winter – just as with humans.

Getting paid
There're no fundamental rules for getting paid, but I have some tips. Generally, it comes down to agreeing

on what suits each client and you, the dog walker. I prefer to get paid weekly but have clients who pay monthly, especially if I walk their dogs just once a week. Cash or bank transfer is the only way you get paid nowadays. Bank transfer is the most common form of payment, especially now that everything is contactless. Some people don't use cash anymore.

Before you walk the dog, make sure you agree on how and when you will get paid before starting.

What do you do if a client forgets to pay? Invoices are probably the best and most professional way to get paid and remind the client to pay you and how much they owe you. Clients don't like being reminded that they've forgotten to pay you, it embarrasses them, and you can lose points for it - an invoice can avoid that.

I've never had problems with not being paid. The only time I might stress would be if the bill began to add up over time and became extensive, it might be difficult for the client to pay, but I've never had this problem. Just make sure you note down all your incomings for your tax returns.

Taking time off

Let clients know as soon as you want to take time off. The longer the notice, the better and ideally, a couple of months or more in advance.

Clients will then have plenty of time to make alternative arrangements, and it gives you time to put money aside (if needed) when you're not working. For example, I take two weeks off over

Christmas and New Year as most clients are off that time, so they don't miss me much, and I wouldn't be earning a full wage either.

If you offer dog walking, you can take any time of the year off, but it's a bit more complicated if you provide to board too. If you offer to board, then a good time to take a break is just before the school summer holidays, as it will help prepare you for the busy time ahead with lots of dogs coming to stay.

School holidays are peak times of the year to board, so you will want to avoid taking time off then. If you have your own family and want to get away, book the last two weeks of the school summer holidays as that's the quietest time. Everyone wants to get away in the first few weeks of school finishing.

Other busy times for boarding dogs are the half-terms in February and October and then Easter. It's so easy to find yourself overworked and working seven days a week. For example, a client may request a dog walk over the weekend to go to the office, and then other clients hear about this and want you to walk their dog so they can take the kids out. Before you know it, you are working seven days a week. It won't take long before you are burnt out and miserable in your new job.

It's not that the weekends will be busy – you might only have one walk with one dog. It's more the physiological effect of knowing that you are working that day, that you are not off, that the day is not your own to do with as you please. We all need that time off to get some R&R and some "me time".

And we all need something to look forward to, even if it's just a weekend in our underpants watching Netflix, eating takeaway. You can't be a good dog walker burnt out and sick of it. Taking weekends off won't damage your business, and you will be a better dog walker for it.

Skye chasing Daisy and Brodie

Dog walking post Covid

2020 changed things quite a bit. For those that continued to work that year, we found ourselves not to be the essential service we had been before. Everyone was either furloughed or working at home. But with nowhere to go and stuck at home, people went out walking locally in the beautiful weather. There was a massive surge in people buying puppies and in 2021-22 requests for dog walkers went through the roof!

I've never seen so much work for dog walkers in 12 years of dog walking, never had so many requests in my whole career. But unfortunately, there are currently not enough dog walkers in the UK at this moment in time.

Closing Words

There is plenty of work, but getting clients can still take time as getting known can take time. Focus on puppy services along with your dog walking to help get clients in – established dog walkers like myself don't have the time for puppy care.

Group dog walking is where you make your money. Three group walks a day (6 dogs in each walk) is enough work for most dog walkers – all in all, a dog walker can earn around £500+ plus a week from that alone once you are full or close to being so (more if you live in London).

Remember to take regular days off, and holiday time so you don't burn out.

Dog boarding can complement your dog walking and pays well (mainly over school holidays). Many dog walking clients look for it when choosing a dog walker.

Doggy daycare in your own home can bring in a substantial additional income or be an alternative to dog walking.

If you are after more money than what dog walking or home daycare can bring in. Daycare within appropriately dedicated premises is your answer. A premises that's big enough to allow 20-40+ dogs a day with the help of staff pays big money. But it is a lot more work and requires some investment, and it can be not easy to find a suitable place.

You can offer other services like cat visits in the client's home, but they are unnecessary. Pet taxi is a ridiculous service, don't waste your time. Services like boarding and daycare may require local council licensing, which means you will need an inspection of your home.

Vans are better than cars, but a car will do perfectly fine if equipped correctly and cost less to buy and prepare.

Firstly, get your business on Facebook and get a Google business listing, as these will all get you clients and get a website if you want.

Lovely photos on Facebook will help create that buzz you need when you start and give clients something to share on their walls.

If you want to pay for advertising, choose local online advertising using Facebook or Google over printed media any day.

❊　❊　❊

FIRST AID FOR DOGS

Introduction

Accidents happen, and illness can occur anytime, usually in the most inappropriate place or when the cause is no longer apparent. It's important to remember that dogs cannot tell us where the pain is, why it is there or how acute it is. Their only defence is to bite, howl or retreat, especially if trying to help causes more pain and distress.

Many first aid procedures are similar to that practised on humans. So a good first aid box, with some adjustment for our dogs and staying calm, helps a lot.

The objective of any first aid is to preserve life by preventing further injury, relieving pain and recognising the level of discomfort, reducing the risk of infection, promoting recovery, and transporting to a veterinary surgeon as soon as possible if required.

Triage

A high or altered breathing rate is a good indicator that something is amiss. Poisons, fevers, seizures, stress and pain can all increase or decrease the normal rate, which should be between 10 and 15 per minute, depending on the condition of the dog. To check the inhalation rate, place hands on ribcage and count for 20 seconds then multiply by 3 to get a rate per minute. The rate should be constant and even with no holding of breath or episodes of panting. If it is not even, then there are problems elsewhere and further checks are required.

By knowing what the dogs pulse rate at rest is then any abnormality is noticeable. The average pulse rate is 60 to 100 heartbeats per minute, depending on the condition of the dog. The easiest place to check the pulse is under the armpit or at the bottom of the ear canal. Count for 20 seconds and multiply by 3 to get the rate per minute. A rate that is not fluent and even signifies a blood pressure problem and will need checking every 3 minutes whilst carrying out any other procedure or during transport to a veterinary surgeon; who will require the information before treatment can commence.

Low blood pressure can be monitored by testing the response of the capillary refill reflex; this is done by gently pressing the gums, which will pale, and seeing how quickly they return to a healthy pink when removing pressure.

Temperature fluctuation can be a result of the dog

going into or being in shock, usually a low reading, fever, influenza or other infectious disease, acute pain or an increase in toxicity levels, usually a high reading. The temperature is taken by inserting a sterilized, greased rectal thermometer into the anus for 2 minutes. A normal temperature is between 100.5°C to 102.5°C. Danger level is anything below 98°, when external warmth should be applied or 103.5° when cooling down is required, by fanning, bathing the paws with cool water or applying ice wrapped in a bag or towel. Water or ice should not be given unless dehydration is suspected, as the dog may have to undergo anaesthesia.

Cuts and Wounds

These usually occur on the feet from running over broken glass or nails, on the head by hitting on a branch or fence bottom or are the result of a fight. Clean the wound with fresh water or a diluted disinfectant such as T.C.P. In addition, apply an antiseptic ointment. Cuts to the pads often bleed profusely, if this is the case apply a pressure bandage to the whole foot, cling film is good for this, ensuring that the blood supply is not cut off. As these wound are usually contaminated check regularly for infection or visit the veterinary surgeon who may prescribe antibiotics. If the bleeding has not stopped in 4 hours then stitches may be required. In extreme emergency, when away from the first aid box, I have used moss and dock leaves to stem the bleeding. A boost to the immune system will help the wound to heal rapidly: I use Selenium and Vitamin E. As the cut heals, I bathe it with extract of Fennel, which relieves irritation, and helps stop the dog chewing at it.

Sting and Insect Bites

Remove sting and if possible determine what type it is. Bee stings and ant bites are acidic and should be bathed with bicarbonate of soda, wasps and jellyfish stings are alkali and should be bathed with vinegar. The most common place is in or on the mouth and the first signs are howls followed by frantic rubbing and rapid swelling of the site. If the swelling is severe and around the nose, muzzle, tongue or throat it can cause breathing difficulties and airways will need to be kept as open as possible until a veterinary surgeon can be seen. If there is no obstruction to the breathing, keep the dog calm, bathe with the above if the type of sting is known, or ice cold water if not. 'Piriton' tablets of 1x 4mg for a small dog, 3 x 4 mg medium dog, 5 x 4mg large dog, will help to reduce the swelling; by assisting in fighting the allergic reaction, and will also help to keep the dog calm.

Lameness

A severe none weight bearing lameness is usually a fracture. If it is less severe, check pads for embedded objects such as tack, nails, thorns, stones, ice, grit, and cut or damaged nails. If the dog is licking or chewing at the foot, it is a good indication that that is the site of the problem and treat as for cuts and wounds. If the problem has been a stone, ice or grit in between the pads they may have been splayed and localised bruising will be apparent. I apply witch-hazel gel and rest the dog for 24 hours. If the dog is not chewing at the foot then the problem is higher up the leg or thigh, usually a strained muscle or ligament that will heal with rest. St. Johns Wort is a good natural painkiller and garlic or liquorish are good anti-inflammatories.

Fractured or Torn Claws

These are very sore and can become infected. If possible, trim the claw of broken or split nail and remove jagged edges. Treat as for wounds, especially if bleeding profusely, if the claw is torn at the base or out of the pad then it will require surgical removal, tape into place using the next claw as support, bandage the whole foot and take the dog to the veterinary surgeon. Dewclaws are most susceptible to being torn, in which case tape down against the leg, bandage and take the dog to the veterinary surgeon. The claw should not be removed without professional help as the bleeding can be very severe and the risk of serious infection is high.

Fits and Seizures

An epileptic seizure is a sign of a malfunction in the brain. It is caused by sudden, uncontrolled activity of neurons and can be triggered by various influences. Different types of seizures represent different degrees of brain activity; commonly classified as either generalized or partial seizures.

Any dog suffering a fit or seizure should be checked out by a veterinary surgeon to determine cause.

The most important thing to remember is that if a dog is having a fit then no restraint should be made. Move any obstacles, darken the room and remain quiet in order not to stimulate the attack.

If the dog has not regained consciousness or has a series of fits over a short time then an emergency visit to the veterinary surgeon is necessary.

Ears

If the dog suddenly develops a sore ear; the usual symptoms are shaking the head or pawing and rubbing the ear, then the most likely cause is a seed or insect that has entered the ear. Remove the foreign object carefully, check for stings and bites and if apparent treat as above. If the problem develops over a period of time then there may be a build up of ear wax, which gentle cleansing with a commercial ear cleaner, vals potion or Almond Oil and vitamin E will solve, or an ear infection such as ear mites which may require more specialised treatment. If the ear has been torn, then clean with disinfectant, apply antibiotic, turn inside out and place over the head and bandage by wrapping around jaw and across the top of the head.

Eyes

If not a general condition such as conjunctivitis, entropion etc. then a topical injury, grass seed, thorns or a toxin may be present. These may scratch the eye causing the cornea to ulcerate so the most important thing is to stop the dog from rubbing the eye. Flush the eye out with a solution of 'Optrex' or lukewarm water. If the problem persists or there is bleeding then take to a veterinary surgeon as soon as possible. If the offending object is removed without damage then bathing with extract of cucumber or tea will help irritation.

Vomiting and Diarrhoea

This is usually a sign that the dog's natural mechanisms have become activated in order to expel something disagreeable from the gut. Starve the dog for 12 hours; ensure there is plenty of clean water or 'Dioralyte' to drink. If the problem persists for more than 3 days or there is lethargy, cramping, blood in the stools or the dog is not drinking then a check up at the veterinary surgery is required.

Heatstroke, Sunburn, Scalds and Burns

Longhaired dogs or dogs with restricted breathing passages such as Boxers can easily over heat on hot days when running around or it can happen when any dog is left in a car or an enclosed kennel.

The early symptoms are excessive panting and breathing difficulties, which can progress to collapse and/or seizure. The dog should be removed from the sun or calmed down, wrapped in cold towels or bathed in cool water, fanned and given plenty of clean water to drink. Exposed areas such as the nose, ear tips or where the fur is thin can have an application of a high factor, anti allergic sun cream or sun block to prevent sunburn. If the area is burnt, ensure the dog has plenty to drink, put an ice pack to the burnt area and apply a soothing lotion such as calamine. If blistering occurs, then lightly bandage and check for infection regularly.

Poisoning

Dogs will eat anything at least once. If the taking in of a toxic substance is suspected then the dog needs to vomit very quickly: unless it is a liquid such as bleach, which will require a veterinary surgeon, as bringing it back up will cause more damage. Most poisons will take 2 hours to have an effect but the less that gets into the system the better. My father always used suspended charcoal but i prefer baking soda placed on the back of the tongue until swallowed or retching commences – mustard powder is preferred by many or mustard paste – right at the back of the gullet. Salt water can be used but is not as quick and 2 or 3 cupfuls may be required. If no side effects are apparent after 2 hours, make sure the dog has plenty to drink and the natural defence mechanism will do the rest. Do not feed for 12 hours and then add immune boosters to the diet in the form of natural enzymes, garlic, Selenium and Vitamin E.

Fractures, Collapse, Trauma Care and Transport

Severe non-weight bearing lameness is usually a fractured limb. This is extremely painful so a painkiller, if available, is required. I use St Johns Wort. The affected limb should be touched as little as possible and first aid treatment needs to be done as calmly and as quickly as possible to limit the distress.

Fractures of the bones below the elbow in the front legs, or knee in the back legs need to be splinted immediately at the accident site. This ensures that the joints above and below the brake is immobilised until the veterinary surgeon can set the fracture properly. The broken ends should be brought together and fixed so that the joint remains formed. If the fracture is in the foreleg then the best splint is a rolled up newspaper formed into a suitable shape and placed around the fracture site, a stick, light strips of metal or cardboard can also be used. Tape the splint in place above and below the fracture with bandage or plaster ensuring the splint is positioned one joint below and above the injury. If the fracture is in a rear limb and below the knee splint together using a material that can form the shape of the natural joint (I once used a car aerial padded with seat foam) and immobilise against the upper limb, again ensuring the splint is positioned below and above the injury.

Fractures of the upper rear leg are more difficult and require expertise, it is better to immobilise and transport the dog for professional treatment. If there is a spinal injury or the dog has collapsed for other reasons then movement should be avoided if possible. Lay the dog on a firm flat surface, such as a wooden board or collapsed cardboard box, as gently as possible, grabbing the skin at the back of the neck and the bottom of the back, slide the dog on to the surface keeping the back and neck straight, then tie firmly into place. If possible, carry carefully to transport, place board flat and go to the veterinary surgery. Be aware that the dog may vomit or defecate, even if unconscious, so another person requires being present. If the dog is in no or little pain, but cannot move limbs or responds to toes being pinched, then it is likely that the spine is broken and the surgeon should be called to the site. Keep the dog warm and calm until he can be sedated.

First aid checklist

Alcohol wipes, Almond oil, Antiseptic, Arnica, Baby Kaolin, Blood Clot Powder, Calamine, Cold Pack, Cotton Balls, Clove Oil, Current food Supplements, Gauze Pads, Gloves, Golden Eye Ointment, Hot Pack, Knife, Nail Clippers, Needle and Stitching, Piriton (Falkor's Pen + Tabs.), Plastic Bags, Q Tips, Saline Solution & Eye Bath, Salt, Scissors (2), Socks, Splints, St. Johns Wortm, Sulphide Ointment, Tape, Thermometer, Tweezers, Vaseline, Vet Wrap, Water

Steriliser Tabs, Wipes, Witch-Hazel

TREAT RECIPE FOR DOG WALKING

Dried Liver

You cant better this dog treat. I use liver for treats when I'm walking all my dogs. There is a vast difference in how the pups respond to these compared to processed shop-bought stuff, and if you do this, you will see why they're the best dog walking treats you can get!

It's very cheap to buy liver from your local supermarket or butcher (much more affordable than branded treats and better for your dog). I cannot emphasize enough how much dogs love these. They are ideal for training, getting the dog's attention, and getting control back when you are outside.

Ingredients
1 packet of liver

Method

1. Get yourself some liver. Any liver will do.

2. Rinse the blood of the liver

3. Wrap a baking tray in kitchen foil - saves a lot of cleaning.

4. Lay your liver on the tray. Preheat your oven to 120c (250f/Gas mark 1). Cook for 1½ - 2 hrs or until liver is fully dry.

5. Cut into little squares and fridge what you will use in a few days and freeze the rest.

Brodie, Flo and Ruby sit for a treat

DOG WALKING CONTRACT

The parties to this contract and agreement are:

Client Name:

Address:

(Hereinafter referred to as "the Owner")

AND

Dog Walker Name:

Address:

(Hereinafter referred to as "the Walker")

The parties choose the above stated addresses as their physical addresses at which legal proceedings may be instituted.

Whereas the Owner wishes to engage the Walker and the Walker agrees to undertake the services under the terms and provisions defined in this Dog Walking Contract as well as the Pet and Owner's information(s) and the Veterinary Release Form which shall all become part of this Contract. Any reference to dogs or pets in this contract shall refer to those specified on the Pet Information sheet(s).

Compensation

The Walker shall be paid the amount per walk:

Duration

This Dog Walking Contract shall come into effect on the date:

And Shall:

A. Terminate on the date:

OR

B. Terminate when either party gives 7 (seven) days written notice of termination.

Cancellation or Early Termination

Either party may terminate this Dog Walking Contract a minimum of 24 (twenty four) hours prior to the first scheduled visit without incurring penalties or damages.

Cancellation by the Owner of scheduled walks with less than 24 hrs notice may be charged at the full rate or rescheduled at the discretion of the Walker.

Should any dog become aggressive or dangerous, the Walker may terminate this dog walking contract with immediate effect.

Any wrongful or misleading information in the Pet and Owner's information sheets may constitute a breach of terms of this Dog Walking Contract and be grounds for instant termination thereof.

Liability

The Walker accepts no liability for any breach of security or loss of or damage to the Owner's property if any other person has access to the property during the term of this agreement.

The Walker shall not be liable for any mishap of whatsoever nature which may befall a dog or caused by a dog who has unsupervised access to the outdoors.

The Owner shall be liable for all medical expenses and damages resulting from an injury to the Walker caused by the dog as well as damage to the Owner's property.

The Walker is released from all liability related to transporting dog(s) to and from any veterinary clinic or kennel, the medical treatment of the dog(s) and the expense thereof.

Indemnification

The Owner will not blame and payback the Walker against any and all costs, expenses, losses, liabilities and claims arising from said dogs behaviour unless the dog walker is willful or negligent.

Emergencies

In the event of an emergency, the Walker shall contact the Owner at the numbers provided to confirm the Owner's choice of action. If the Owner cannot be reached timeously, the Walker is authorized to:

Transport the dog(s) to the listed veterinarian;

Request on-site treatment from a veterinarian;

Transport the dog(s) to an emergency clinic if the previous two options are not feasible.

Security

The Walker warrants to keep safe and confidential all keys, remote control entry devices, access codes and personal information of the Owner and to return same to the Owner at the end of the contract period or immediately upon demand.

Whole Agreement

This Dog Walking Contract and Pet and Owner's

information sheet(s) and the Veterinary Release Form attached constitute the sole and entire agreement between the parties with regard to the subject matter hereof and the parties waive the right to rely on any alleged expressed or implied provision not contained therein. Any alteration to this agreement must be in writing and signed by both parties.

Assignment

No party may assign any of its rights or delegate or assign any of its obligations in terms of this Dog Walking Contract without the prior written consent of the other party, except where otherwise stated.

Walking dogs off lead

If agreed to by the Owner, the Walker has permission to walk the dog(s) off lead. By doing so, the Walker agrees to only walk the dog(s) off lead at safe and appropriate times and places.

Authorisation to walk dog(s) off the lead: Yes/No

Authorisation to walk dog(s) with other dogs: Yes/No

Signed by the Owner who warrants his/her authority to enter into this agreement

Date of Signature:

Signed by the Walker who warrants his/her authority to enter into this agreement

Date of Signature:

PET AND OWNER'S INFO SHEET

Pet 1:
Pet's Name:
Pet's DOB:
Breed:
Sex:
Spayed/Neutred:
Medications:
Date of last vaccination:
Owners signature:

Pet 2:
Pet's Name:
Pet's DOB:
Breed:
Sex:
Spayed/Neutred:
Medications:
Date of last vaccination:
Owners signature:

Owner's Information
Name:
Address:
Phone Number:
Work Number:
Emergency Contact:

Emergency Number:

VETERINARY RELEASE FORM

Owner's Name:
Address:
Phone Number:
Work Number:

Pet 1 Name:
Description:
DOB:
Medications:
Microchip Number:

Pet 2 Name:
Description:
DOB:
Medications:
Microchip Number:

If any of the pets named above becomes ill or is
injured, I request _____take the pets to:
Veterinary Office Name:
Address:
Phone Number:
Pet Insurance No:
Policy Company:

TO WHOM IT MAY CONCERN

I hereby authorize the attending veterinarian to treat any of my pets as listed above and I accept full responsibility for all fees and charges incurred in the treatment of any of my pets.

The Dog Walker is authorized to transport my pet(s) to and from the veterinary clinic for treatment or to request "on-site" treatment if deemed necessary. If I cannot be reached in case of an emergency, the walker shall act on my behalf to authorize any treatment excluding euthanasia.

I give permission to approve treatment up to £1,000. I will assume full responsibility upon my return for payment and/or reimbursement for veterinary services rendered up to the above stated amount.

Dog walker – Full Name:

Dog walker – Signature:

Dog Owner's Signature:

Date:

THANK YOU FOR BUYING MY BOOK

Me and the dogs finishing up a walk

OTHER BOOKS BY THIS AUTHOR

Dog Food & Treat Recipes

Available on Amazon

Some of the most popular dog food and treat recipes in the UK. Including the world's first-ever guide on dehydrating treats for dogs. An ideal gift.
https://amzn.to/3rVSYAn

Printed in Great Britain
by Amazon

17938007R00047